Mispelled or Misspelled?

Mispelled or Misspelled?

by

James J. Magee

ISBN: 1-58820-096-5

1stBooks - rev. 7/10/00

Introduction

Misspell or Misspell? was not written so you could correct spelling errors per se; you have spell checker on your computer for that purpose. This book was written so you could spell words correctly and with confidence the first time you wrote them. The best method for using this learning tool is to try a page a day with a piece of scrap paper [answer sheet] on the side. Soon, you will be able to confidently spell the most commonly misspelled words correctly the first time you write them.

mispelled or misspelled

ukalele or ukulele

inheritence or inheritance

disappointment or dissappointment

daugther or daughter

personnel or personell

consumate or consummate

reassess or reasess

sargeant or sergeant

colonel or colonal

gratful or grateful

splender or splendor

repetition or repitition

utterance or utterence

embarass or embarrass

misspelled

ukulele

inheritance

disappointment

daughter

personnel

consummate

reassess

sergeant

colonel

grateful

splendor

repetition

utterance

embarrass

brilliance or brillance

audience or audiance

awareness or awarness

fiesty or feisty

socialy or socially

complication or complacation

postpone or pospone

celler or cellar

iregular or irregular

playwright or playright

annulled or annuled

actualy or actually

traped or trapped

unwarranted or unwaranted

adoptian or adoption

brilliance

audience

awareness

feisty

socially

complication

postpone

cellar

irregular

playwright

annulled

actually

trapped

unwarranted

adoption

valiant or valient

acknowledge or aknowledge

dispicable or despicable

occurring or occuring

miget or midget

kaleidoscope or kalidoscope

transparant or transparent

grusome or gruesome

abundant or abundent

injurous or injurious

offence or offense

defence or defense

codecil or codicil

committ or commit

advertise or advertize

valiant

acknowledge

despicable

occurring

midget

kaleidoscope

transparent

gruesome

abundant

injurious

both

defense

codicil

commit

both

vilainous or villainous

worshipped or worshiped

tormenter or tormentor

occurs or occurrs

escapes or ecsapes

grueling or gruelling

annulment or annullment

challenge or challange

stopped or stoped

talketive or talkative

druged or drugged

physican or physician

apparently or apparantly

wilfully or willfully

stevadore or stevedore

villainous

both

both

occurs

escape

both

annulment

challenge

stopped

talkative

drugged

physician

apparently

willfully

stevedore

strenght or strength

disturbance or disturbence

extremly or extremely

employe or employee

dispel or disspel

disapproval or dissapproval

occuppied or occupied

llulaby or lullaby

pastor or paster

gambler or gamblor

wilful or willful

seranade or serenade

celibacy or celebacy

collegues or colleagues

jeopardy or jeoperdy

strength

disturbance

extremely

both

dispel

disapproval

occupied

lullaby

pastor

gambler

willful

serenade

celibacy

colleagues

jeopardy

ingredient or ingrediant

neice or niece

nuptial or nuptuil

incompetence or incompetance

referrel or referral

repentence or repentance

mariner or marinor

coordinater or coordinator

suave or sauve

reverance or reverence

trekked or treked

phamplets or pamphlets

vengence or vengeance

scoundral or scoundrel

importance or importence

ingredient

niece

nuptial

incompetence

referral

repentance

mariner

coordinator

suave

reverence

trekked

pamphlet

vengeance

scoundrel

importance

newphew or nephew

banistor or banister

enoble or ennoble

earing or earring

unconquorable or unconquerable

tragedy or trajedy

beginner or beginer

occured or occurred

decsent or descent

malignant or malignant

compliance or complience

depressed or depresed

diarrhea or diarhea

perceptable or perceptible

intensely or intensly

nephew

banister

ennoble

earring

unconquerable

tragedy

beginner

occurred

both

malignant

compliance

depressed

diarrhea

perceptible

intensely

judgment or judgement

prerogative or perogative

tarriff or tariff

dominance or dominence

finesse or fenesse

easal or easel

repellent or repellant

journel or journal

dissiminate or disseminate

preferred or perferred

botany or boteny

wetter or wetier

proceed or procede

boundries or boundaries

marriage or marraige

both

prerogative

tariff

dominance

finesse

easel

repellent

journal

disseminate

preferred

botany

wetter

proceed

boundaries

marriage

manageable or manageble

bankrupcy or bankruptcy

valleys or vallies

picnicking or picknicing

receipt or reciept

dynamos or dynamoes

hieght or height

plagiarize or plagerize

allegience or allegiance

stanima or stamina

attorney or attornay

occassionally or occasionally

succeed or suceed

sucess or success

sucessful or successful

manageable

bankruptcy

valleys

picnicking

receipt

dynamos

height

plagiarize

allegiance

stamina

attorney

occasionally

succeed

success

successful

difference or differance

conveniance or convenience

convenient or conveniant

differant or different

discription or description

arguement or argument

imaginary or imaginery

descendant or descendent

performance or preformance

discend or descend

parliment or parliament

villein or villain

resturant or restaurant

possess or posess

professor or professer

difference

convenience

convenient

different

description

argument

imaginary

both

performance

descend

parliament

villain

restaurant

possess

professor

government or goverment

laboratory or laborotory

acquaint or aquaint

truely or truly

accidentally or accidently

accomodate or accommodate

acquaintance or acquaintence

abominable or abominible

artic or arctic

belligerant or belligerent

benevolent or benevelent

chocolate or chockolate

characteristic or charactoristic

cruelty or crulty

evory or every

government

laboratory

acquaint

truly

accidentally

accommodate

acquaintance

abominable

arctic

belligerent

benevolent

chocolate

characteristic

cruelty

every

address or adress

aggrevate or aggravate

all right or alright

amataur or amateur

believed or beleived

committee or comittee

competition or compitition

conscientious or conscientous

conscious or concious

cooly or coolly

deceive or decieve

dineing or dining

doesn't or dosen't

eight or eigth

exersise or exercise

address

aggravate

all right

amateur

believed

committee

competition

conscientious

conscious

coolly

deceive

dining

doesn't

eight

exercise

schedule or skedule

separate or seperate

abestos or asbestos

superintendant or superintendent

Wedesday or Wednesday

auxillary or auxiliary

buoyent or buoyant

catelogue or catalogue

carreer or career

comptroler or comptroller

criticise or criticize

dividend or dividand

expedient or expediant

inviegle or inveigle

monetary or monetery

schedule

separate

asbestos

superintendent

Wednesday

auxiliary

buoyant

catalogue

career

comptroller

criticize

dividend

expedient

inveigle

monetary

resistance or resistence

collapable or collapsible

confectionary or confectionery

invidous or invidious

hymenal or hymeneal

concomitant or concommitant

coherence or coherance

feasible or feaseble

touchible or touchable

portentious or portentous

monogomy or monogamy

malfeasence or malfeasance

enforceable or enforcible

adaptable or adaptible

adjustible or adjustable

resistance

collapsible

confectionery

invidious

hymeneal

concomitant

coherence

feasible

touchable

portentous

monogamy

malfeasance

enforceable

adaptable

adjustable

technicality or technicallity

tendancy or tendency

thier or their

thousandth or thousendth

transfered or transferred

transiant or transient

yield or yeild

inocuous or innocuous

inoculate or innoculate

harass or harrass

inuendo or innuendo

dessicate or desiccate

mimmicing or mimicking

nemonic or mnemonic

correllation or correlation

technicality

tendency

their

thousandth

transferred

transient

yield

innocuous

inoculate

harass

innuendo

desiccate

mimicking

mnemonic

correlation

joys or joyies

potatos or potatoes

banjoes or banjos

wifes or wives

halfs or halves

shelves or shelfs

misread or missread

oxes or oxen

churches or churchs

elfs or elves

enemy or enimies

screechs or screeches

foxes or foxs

echos or echoes

donkeys or donkies

joys

potatoes

both

wives

halves

shelves

misread

oxen

churches

elves

enemies

screeches

foxes

echoes

donkeys

courts-martial or court-martials

commanders-in-chief or commander-in-chiefs

looker-ons or lookers on

essential or essentiel

superficiel or superficial

commerciel or commercial

senatorial or senatoriel

cowes or cows

mouthfulles or mouthfuls

poisonious or poisonous

ambiguous or ambigous

erronious or erroneous

mismanage or missmanage

spoonfuls or spoonfulls

hideous or hidious

court-martial

commanders-in-chief

lookers-on

essential

superficial

commercial

senatorial

cows

mouthfuls

poisonous

ambiguous

erroneous

mismanage

spoonfuls

hideous

outragious or outrageous

industreous or industrious

courtious or courteous

victoreous or victorious

deliceous or delicious

gorgious or gorgeous

ambitous or ambitious

envious or enveous

remarcable or remarkable

desirible or desirable

favorible or favorable

misquote or missquote

audable or audible

eligable or eligible

enjoyable or enjoyible

outrageous

industrious

courteous

victorious

delicious

gorgeous

ambitious

envious

remarkable

desirable

favorable

misquote

audible

eligible

enjoyable

apparratus or apparatus

misstuned or mistuned

chargible or chargeable

readable or readible

acceptible or acceptable

callosal or colossal

convertible or convertable

tangable or tangible

contemptable or contemptible

memorible or memorable

resistable or resistible

educible or educable

flexable or flexible

inevitible or inevitable

mislead or misslead

apparatus

mistuned

chargeable

readable

acceptable

colossal

convertible

tangible

contemptible

memorable

resistible

educable

flexible

inevitable

mislead

misslay or mislay

scissors or sciossers

column or colunm

catagory or category

misfile or missfile

publacize or publicize

knicknack or knickknack

eminance or eminence

preference or preferance

hemorhage or hemorrhage

encite or incite

eleven or elevan

ramed or rammed

labelled or labeled

prairie or praire

mislay

scissors

column

category

misfile

publicize

knickknack

eminence

preference

hemorrhage

incite

eleven

rammed

both

prairie

realizing or realaizing

workkshop or workshop

chandalier or chandelier

alocate or allocate

cancelation or cancellation

missinform or misinform

strengthen or strenghten

insistant or insistent

ectasy or ecstasy

ranced or rancid

indeleble or indelible

ennable or enable

grandeur or grandaur

misinterpret or missinterpret

irrefutable or irrefutible

realizing

workshop

chandelier

allocate

cancellation

misinform

strengthen

insistent

ecstacy

rancid

indelible

enable

grandeur

misinterpret

irrefutable

depository or deposatory

computer or computor

contractor or contracter

delagate or delegate

breakage or breakege

operator or operater

decrepet or decrepit

indubitable or indubitible

delete or delite

hypocrit or hypocrite

luxurient or luxuriant

gameskeeper or gamekeeper

counterfeitor or counterfeiter

improvise or improvize

chaperone or chaperon

depository

computer

contractor

delegate

breakage

operator

decrepit

indubitable

delete

hypocrite

luxuriant

gamekeeper

counterfeiter

improvise

chaperon

ardor or arder

rachet or rachett

coral or corall

quarrelled or quarreled

ballerina or ballarina

uped or upped

augur or auger

continuously or coninuously

dissected or disected

omalet or omelet

defendant or defedent

inconsistent or inconsistant

orthodox or orthrodox

wolfes or wolves

practising or practicing

ardor

rachet

corral

both

ballerina

upped

augur

continuously

dissected

omelet

defendant

inconsistent

orthodox

wolves

practicing

erasible or erasable

copyright or copywright

whince or wince

biassed or biased

accussation or accusation

existance or existence

conive or connive

asymmetrical or asymetrical

acquire or aquire

remark or remarck

permit or permitt

anciant or ancient

hindrence or hindrance

conquer or conquor

annoyence or annoyance

erasable

copyright

wince

biased

accusation

existence

connive

asymmetrical

acquire

remark

permit

ancient

hinderance

conquer

annoyance

condemn or condemm

command or comand

gluttonous or gluttenous

vicious or vicous

fulness or fullness

persistence or persistance

inappropriate or inapropriate

inopportune or inoportune

confered or conferred

acumulation or accumulation

betrayor or betrayer

sorceress or soceress

machinery or machinary

monastery or monastary

eunuch or eunach

condemn

command

gluttonous

vicious

fullness

persistence

inappropriate

inopportune

conferred

accumulation

betrayer

sorceress

machinery

monastery

eunuch

promenade or promanade

wooly or woolly

supercede or supersede

smoulder or smolder

minstrel or minstral

prominence or prominance

suplant or supplant

fense or fence

parley or parlay

fortell or foretell

achievment or achievement

parlamentarian or parliamentarian

jailer or jailor

razer or razor

tuter or tutor

promenade

both

supersede

both

minstrel

prominence

supplant

fence

both

foretell

achievement

parliamentarian

both

razor

tutor

metalic or metallic

cummerbund or commerbund

instructor or instructer

persistant or persistent

caraciture or caricature

serated or serrated

pizzazz or pizazz

severence or severance

concise or consise

rebeled or rebelled

mischievious or mischievous

legendery or legendary

illegitimate or illigitimate

heritege or heritage

instruement or instrument

metallic

cummerbund

instructor

persistent

caricature

serrated

both

severance

concise

rebelled

mischievous

legendary

illegitimate

heritage

instrument

embody or imbody

embroidery or embroidary

intercede or intersede

reverie or revery

reminised or reminisced

succulant or succulent

oder or odor

mispend or misspend

compell or compel

carousel or carousal

monkeys or monkies

healtiest or healthiest

customary or customery

lampost or lamppost

antecedent or antecedant

embody

embroidery

intercede

both

reminisced

succulent

odor

misspend

compel

both

monkeys

healthiest

customary

lamppost

antecedent

sentence or sentance

battalion or battalian

cemetary or cemetery

forceble or forcible

abeyance or abeyence

grammer or grammar

humor or humour

humorous or humerous

privilege or privilage

defenite or definite

prophesy or prophecy

equiped or equipped

equipment or equippment

business or bussiness

atlethic or athletic

sentence

battalion

cemetery

forcible

abeyance

grammar

both

humorous

privilege

definite

prophecy

equipped

equipment

business

athletics

heros or heroes

familier or familiar

disappear or dissappear

critisism or criticism

certain or certian

necessary or necessery

fascinate or fasinate

recommend or reccomend

benefited or benefitted

studing or studying

extraordinery or extraordinary

February or Februery

grievous or grievious

irrelevent or irrelevant

newstand or newsstand

heroes

familiar

disappear

criticism

certain

necessary

fascinate

recommend

benefitted

studying

extraordinary

February

grievous

irrelevant

newsstand

percolator or perkulator

pimento or pimiento

reconigze or recognize

absance or absence

across or accross

friend or freind

indispensible or indispensable

knowledge or knowledge

maintenance or maintenence

noticeble or noticeable

parallel or parallal

perhapps or perhaps

queit or quiet

rhythmn or rhythm

rhyme or rhymne

percolator

pimento

recognize

absence

across

friend

indispensable

knowledge

maintenance

noticeable

parallel

perhaps

quiet

rhythm

rhyme

municipel or municipal

promotionel or promotional

manuever or maneuver

tranquelity or tranquility

accessible or acessible

restreint or restraint

transferable or transferible

reliance or relience

invulnerable or invulnerible

aberrant or aberrent

dutyies or duties

instantainously or instantaneously

president or presidant

precede or preceed

promissary or promissory

municipal

promotional

maneuver

tranquility

accessible

restraint

transferable

reliance

invulnerable

aberrant

duties

instantaneously

president

precede

promissory

purchasible or purchasable

responsability or responsibility

regrettable or regretable

soceity or society

simplifyed or simplified

hypocrisy or hypocracy

questionnaire or questionaire

misprint or missprint

mantal or mantel

beachs or beaches

bushs or bushes

axs or axes

skies or skys

waltzes or waltzs

opportunities or opportunitys

purchasable

responsibility

regrettable

society

simplified

hypocrisy

questionnaire

misprint

mantel

beaches

bushes

axes

skies

waltzes

opportunities

cellos or celloes

dishes or dishs

thiefs or thieves

buzzs or buzzes

son-in-laws or sons-in-law

advantagious or advantageous

armfuls or armfulls

mispronounce or misspronounce

beautious or beauteous

rebelleous or rebellious

cautious or cauteous

graceous or gracious

gloreous or glorious

mystereous or mysterious

maliceous or malicious

cellos

dishes

thieves

buzzes

sons-in-law

advantageous

armfuls

mispronounce

beauteous

rebellious

cautious

gracious

glorious

mysterious

malicious

rights-of-way or right-of-ways

deferred or defered

editor-in-chiefs or editors-in-chief

passer-bys or passers-by

misplace or missplace

imaginible or imaginable

sensable or sensible

misshape or mishape

incredable or incredible

permissible or permissable

bookeeping or bookkeeping

possable or possible

bribible or bribable

agreeible or agreeable

visable or visible

right-of-ways

deferred

editors-in-chief

passers-by

misplace

imaginable

sensible

misshape

incredible

permissible

bookkeeping

possible

bribable

agreeable

visible

cosher or kosher

laundramat or laundromat

undeniable or undenieble

attendence or attendance

appaling or appalling

overrun or overun

rapturous or rapurous

melancholy or meloncholy

cuthroat or cutthroat

collapse or colapse

pharmecy or pharmacy

mishandle or misshandle

pantomine or pantomime

gpysy or gypsy

vendible or vendable

kosher

laundromat

undeniable

attendance

appalling

overrun

rapturous

melancholy

cutthroat

collapse

pharmacy

mishandle

pantomime

gypsy

vendible

saleable or salable

allowence or allowance

pertinent or pertinant

warrior or warrier

correspondance or correspondence

rarify or rarefy

foundrys or foundries

adapter or adaptor

acclimate or acclimmate

handkerchief or hankerchief

spaghetti or spagetti

kitchen of kitchan

oporation or operation

weasel or weasal

slyer or slier

both

allowance

pertinent

warrior

correspondence

rarefy

foundries

adapter

acclimate

handkerchief

spaghetti

kitchen

operation

weasel

both

helicopter or helocopter

jeopardize of jeopardise

messianic or mesianic

fiancé or fiancée

shanghaid or shanghied

postumously or posthumously

affidavit of afidavit

aquitted or acquitted

governor or governer

seap or seep

roomate or roommate

hietal or hiatal

masquerade or masquarade

serate or serrate

arive or arrive

helicopter

jeopardize

messianic

both

shanghaied

posthumously

affidavit

acquitted

governor

seep

roommate

hiatal

masquerade

serrate

arrive

lien or lein

agresive or aggressive

openess or openness

weild or wield

mishap or misshap

odyssey or oddessy

spector or spectre

knoty or knotty

nightmaresh or nightmarish

tiered or teired

assualt or assault

burgalry or burglary

polution or pollution

contaversy or controversy

contemporary or contemporery

lien

aggressive

openness

wield

mishap

odyssey

both

knotty

nightmarish

tiered

assault

burglary

pollution

controversy

contemporary

adolescent or adolesent

pier or peir

lavatory or lavetory

irregularities or irregularaties

supoenas or subpoenas

fortfeiture or forfeiture

quandry or quandery

discrepancies or discrepencies

emmense or immense

cartilage or cartilege

plaintiff or plaintif

sheriff or sherif

shelter or sheltar

dsolve or dissolve

barbecue or barbeque

adolescent

pier

lavatory

irregularities

subpoenas

forfeiture

quandry

discrepancies

immense

cartilage

plaintiff

sheriff

shelter

dissolve

barbecue

Index

A

B

C

D

E

F

G

H

I

J

K

N

O

P

Q

R

S

T

U

V

W

Y

ABOUT THE AUTHOR

James Magee is a court administrator with a B.A. in Philosophy and a M.A. in Education. His background includes a tour of duty as a Naval Officer in Vietnam and 20 years of service in the New York State civil and courts.

www.ingramcontent.com/pod-product-compliance
Ingram Content Group UK Ltd.
Pitfield, Milton Keynes, MK11 3LW, UK
UKHW041933190726
13854UKWH00004B/1557